D1243690

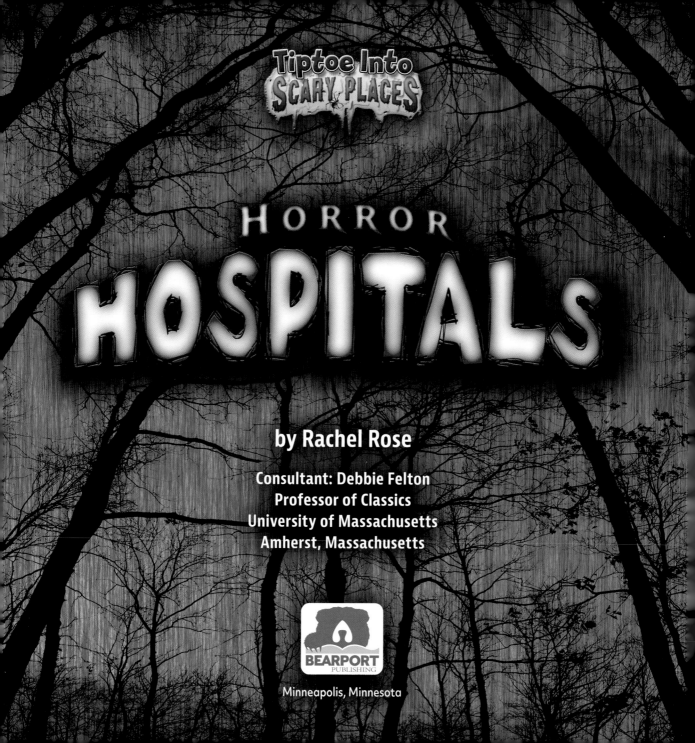

Tiptoe Into SCARY PLACES

HORROR HOSPITALS

by Rachel Rose

Consultant: Debbie Felton
Professor of Classics
University of Massachusetts
Amherst, Massachusetts

BEARPORT
PUBLISHING

Minneapolis, Minnesota

Credits

Cover, © Kim Jones, and © Oksana Mizina/Stutterstock; 3, © Sherman Cahal/Shutterstock; 4-5, © Kim Jones, ©Pakhnyushchy/Stutterstock.com, and ©Kirill Zdorov-stock.adobe.com; 6, © Steve Allen/Shutterstock; 7, © Steve Heap/Shutterstock; 8, © Ten03/Shutterstock; 9, © Amy Cicconi/Alamy; 10, © Alex_F/Shutterstock; 11, © Tony Baggett/Shutterstock; 12, © chippix/Shutterstock; 13, © Sorn340 Images/Shutterstock; 14, © xpixel/Shutterstock; 15, © Pietro Basilico/Shutterstock; 16, © Chalermpon Poungpeth/Shutterstock; 17, © Realy Easy Star/Toni Spagone/Alamy; 18, Wikimedia Commons/Public Domain; 19, © Kevin Lee/Flickr; 20, © Andreas Gradin/Shutterstock; 21, © Kevin Lee/Flickr and © Oote Boe/Alamy; 23, © aswphotos134/Shutterstock; and 24, © Mara Fribus/Shutterstock.

President: Jen Jenson
Director of Product Development: Spencer Brinker
Editor: Allison Juda
Designer: Micah Edel
Cover: Kim Jones

Library of Congress Cataloging-in-Publication Data

Names: Rose, Rachel, 1968– author.—
Title: Horror hospitals / by Rachel Rose.—
Description: Minneapolis, Minnesota : Bearport Publishing Company, [2021] |—
    Series: Tiptoe into scary places | Includes bibliographical references—
    and index.—
Identifiers: LCCN 2020002566 (print) | LCCN 2020002567 (ebook) | ISBN—
    9781647471750 (library binding) | ISBN 9781647471811 (ebook)—
Subjects: LCSH: Haunted hospitals—Juvenile literature.—
Classification: LCC BF1474.4 .R67 2021 (print) | LCC BF1474.4 (ebook) |—
    DDC 133.1/22—dc23
LC record available at https://lccn.loc.gov/2020002566—
LC ebook record available at https://lccn.loc.gov/2020002567

For more information, write to Bearport Publishing, 5357 Penn Avenue South, Minneapolis, MN 55419. Printed in the United States of America.

CONTENTS

HORROR HOSPITALS

It is getting dark and visiting hours are over. You say good night to your friend, a **patient** at the hospital. In the elevator, you press the button for the first floor. But the elevator keeps going—all the way down to the basement. Suddenly, the lights go out!

Get ready to read four spooky
tales about hospitals. Turn the
page . . . if you dare!

TRAGIC TALES

Trans-Allegheny Lunatic Asylum, Weston, West Virginia

The Trans-Allegheny Lunatic Asylum opened in 1864. It was built as a **psychiatric** hospital. Harmful experiments were done on its patients. Some people even died because of these experiments.

The hospital was shut down in 1994, but the building is still there today. And so too, it is said, are the **tormented** souls of the patients. . . .

The Trans-Allegheny
Lunatic Asylum

Lily is one of the ghosts believed to roam the floors of the old hospital building. Lily died when she was only a child. Today, visitors say they can still hear her giggling. Some have seen a ball that rolls by itself. Is Lily looking for someone to play with?

Not all the ghosts at the hospital are as friendly as Lily. Ruth is an angry spirit said to scream, throw things, and even push people!

Inside the asylum

THE HAUNTED ELEVATOR

St. Bartholomew's Hospital, London, England

St. Bartholomew's is England's oldest hospital—nearly 900 years old. It is located in the center of London, and its doctors and nurses are kept very busy. But patients aren't the only ones who take up their time. The hospital's ghostly spirits also need some attention!

The ghost of a crying boy has been seen roaming the hospital halls. Some say when he appears it is an **omen** someone is going to die.

St. Bartholomew's Hospital

11

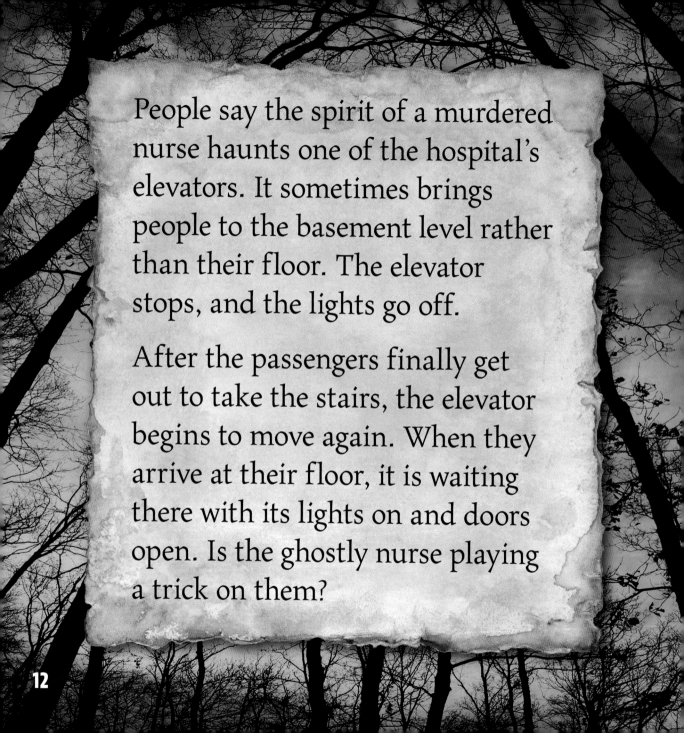

People say the spirit of a murdered nurse haunts one of the hospital's elevators. It sometimes brings people to the basement level rather than their floor. The elevator stops, and the lights go off.

After the passengers finally get out to take the stairs, the elevator begins to move again. When they arrive at their floor, it is waiting there with its lights on and doors open. Is the ghostly nurse playing a trick on them?

ISLAND OF TERROR

Poveglia Island, Venice, Italy

The lonely Poveglia Island lies off the coast of Venice, Italy. In the fourteenth century, thousands of people who were ill from the **bubonic plague** were taken there to die. After they died, many of the bodies were burned. It is said only half the island is made of soil. The other half is human ash!

Poveglia Island

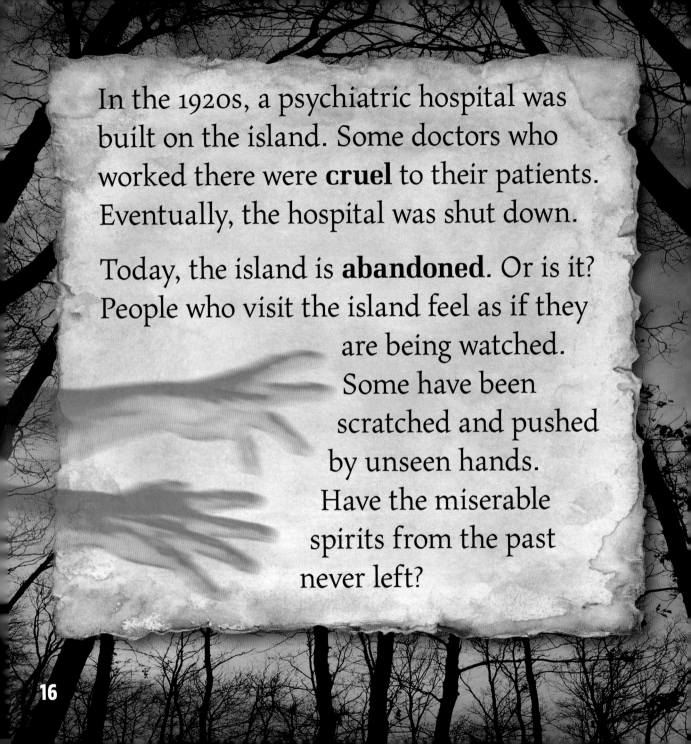

In the 1920s, a psychiatric hospital was built on the island. Some doctors who worked there were **cruel** to their patients. Eventually, the hospital was shut down.

Today, the island is **abandoned**. Or is it? People who visit the island feel as if they are being watched. Some have been scratched and pushed by unseen hands. Have the miserable spirits from the past never left?

The Bell Tower on Poveglia Island

One story tells of a cruel doctor who went mad. One day, he fell from the bell tower and died. Did the spirits of his **tortured** victims push him?

PRISONERS OF WAR

Old Changi Hospital, Changi Village, Singapore

The Old Changi (CHANG-ee) Hospital was built in 1935. It was captured by the Japanese when they invaded Singapore during World War II (1939–1945). They turned the hospital into a prison camp. Many people were tortured and died there. The hospital closed down in 1997.

An illustration of prisoners in Changi

Inside Old Changi Hospital

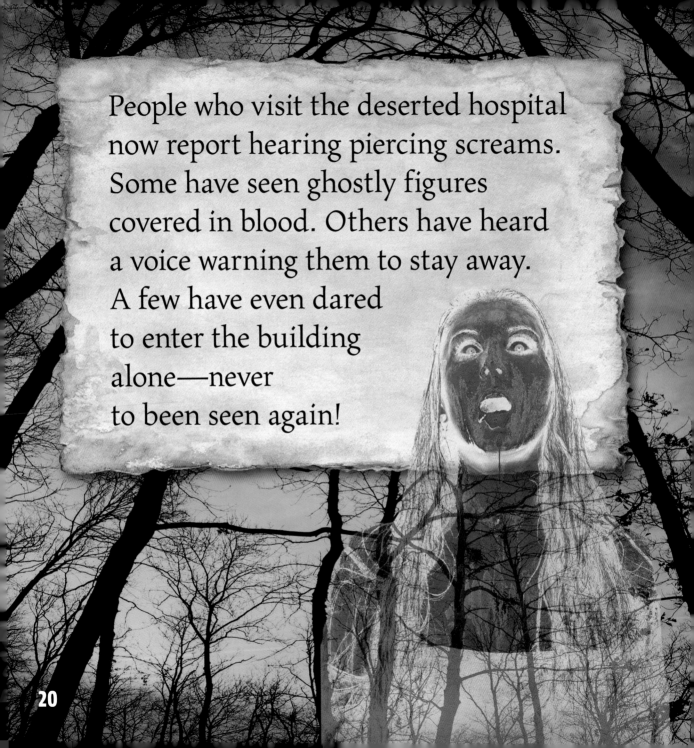

People who visit the deserted hospital now report hearing piercing screams. Some have seen ghostly figures covered in blood. Others have heard a voice warning them to stay away. A few have even dared to enter the building alone—never to been seen again!

In 2017, a frightening video appeared on the internet. It showed a mysterious nurse carrying a baby and walking through the empty hospital.

HORROR HOSPITALS
AROUND THE WORLD

TRANS-ALLEGHENY LUNATIC ASYLUM
Weston, West Virginia

Meet a phantom child looking for a playmate.

ST. BARTHOLOMEW'S HOSPITAL
London, England

Take a ride in England's most haunted elevator.

POVEGLIA ISLAND
Venice, Italy

What lurks in the haunted **ruins** of a deserted island?

OLD CHANGI HOSPITAL
Changi Village, Singapore

Visit an abandoned hospital . . . at your own risk.

Arctic Ocean

NORTH AMERICA

EUROPE

ASIA

Atlantic Ocean

AFRICA

Pacific Ocean

Pacific Ocean

SOUTH AMERICA

Indian Ocean

Atlantic Ocean

AUSTRALIA

Southern Ocean

ANTARCTICA

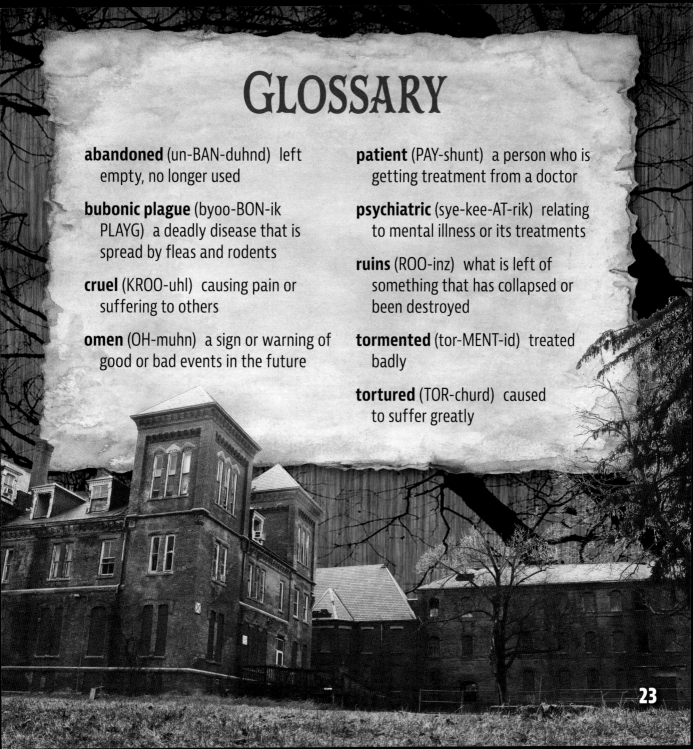

GLOSSARY

abandoned (un-BAN-duhnd) left empty, no longer used

bubonic plague (byoo-BON-ik PLAYG) a deadly disease that is spread by fleas and rodents

cruel (KROO-uhl) causing pain or suffering to others

omen (OH-muhn) a sign or warning of good or bad events in the future

patient (PAY-shunt) a person who is getting treatment from a doctor

psychiatric (sye-kee-AT-rik) relating to mental illness or its treatments

ruins (ROO-inz) what is left of something that has collapsed or been destroyed

tormented (tor-MENT-id) treated badly

tortured (TOR-churd) caused to suffer greatly

INDEX

READ MORE

Williams, Dinah. *Abandoned Insane Asylums (Scary Places).* New York: Bearport (2008).

Williams, Dinah. *Shuttered Horror Hospitals (Scary Places).* New York: Bearport (2011).

LEARN MORE ONLINE

1. Go to **www.factsurfer.com**
2. Enter "**Horror Hospitals**" into the search box.
3. Click on the cover of this book to see a list of websites.

ABOUT THE AUTHOR

Rachel Rose writes books for children and teaches yoga. She lives in San Francisco with her husband and her dog, Sandy.